Y0-EKQ-460

3

RULES THAT GUARANTEE FINANCIAL SUCCESS

From the Author of *425 Ways to Stretch Your $$$$*

Vernon Williams

Empowerment Publishers

Columbia, Maryland

Library of Congress Cataloging-in-Publication Data

Williams, Vernon

3 Rules that Guarantee Financial Success/ Vernon Williams

ISBN 0-9777338-6-6

Published by Empowerment Publishers.

Copyright © 2008 by Vernon Williams. All rights reserved. No Part of this book shall be reproduced or transmitted in any form or by any means, electronic, mechanical, magnetic, photographic, including photocopying, recording or by any information storage and retrieval system, without the prior written permission of the publisher. No patent liability is assumed with respect to the use of the information contained herein. Although every precaution has been taken in the preparation of this book, the publisher and author assume no responsibility for errors or omissions. Neither is any liability assumed for damages resulting from the use of the information contained herein.

This book is available at quantity discounts with bulk purchases. For more information, please visit
www.howtocutyourexpenses.com

OTHER BOOKS BY VERNON WILLIAMS

- 425 Ways to Stretch Your $$$$

- Paddle Your Own Boat: 10 Rules that Guarantee Career Success

- Why Employees Fail to Meet Performance Expectations & How to Fix the Problem

Available at www.howtocutexpenses.com

TABLE OF CONTENTS

PREFACE

Do you live paycheck to paycheck? According to the American Payroll Association, 67% of American workers do. That does not have to be the truth for you.

Having been a personal finance educator for more than 20 years, I have identified the key steps people who are financially successful follow. I share those with you in this practical workbook.

Best wishes to you as you travel the road to financial success.

1

SET GOALS

As Jim Rohn says: "The future does not get better by **hope**, it gets better by **planning**. Planning means having **goals**."

Benefits of goals:

- Motivation – They get you moving
- Movement is **focused** in a predetermined direction
- Less stress
- Higher achievement

Use the **SMART** method to set goals:

Specific

The goal should be precise rather than vague.

Examples:

- o Establish an emergency fund.
- o Establish a 401(k) Plan.

Measurable

Making your goal measurable helps you see your progress, determine if you are moving in the right direction, and see how far you still need to go.

Examples:

- o Direct **10%** of my income into an emergency fund each month.
- o Deposit **5%** of my income into a 401(k) plan each month.

Achievable

It doesn't have to be easy, but you must have a reasonable chance of achieving the goal. That means having the desire, income and discipline.

Relevant

The goal should be meaningful and make a difference in your life.

Time Definite

Set a specific time by which you expect to achieve the goal. This adds an element of urgency and motivation.

> Examples:
>
> o   Beginning **June 2009** and continuing until the balance reaches 3 months of living expense.
>
> o   By **January 2010**.

See a sample of a completed Goals Worksheet on page 4.

SAMPLE GOALS WORKSHEET

(**S**pecific) I will <u>buy my first home</u>.

(**M**easurable) I will have succeeded when <u>I move into my new home</u>.

(**A**chievable) I have the following **r**esources: <u>$1,000 in savings, a well-paying job, and good credit</u>. I will take the following action:

Action	Complete by
1. Determine how much I can afford	9/08
2. Attend a new homebuyer seminar	10/08
3. Review my credit report	10/08
4. Research down payment assistance programs	11/08
4. Shop for a loan	1/09
5. Shop for a home	2/09-3/09
6. Make an offer	4/09
7. Get a home inspection	4/09
8. Shop for homeowners insurance	5/09
9. Sign papers	5/09
10. Move into my new home	6/09

(**R**elevant) This goal is meaningful to me because <u>I am building wealth</u>.

(**T**ime Definite) I will have achieved my goal by <u>June 2009</u>.

Activity

Use the SMART method to list your goal on the Goals Worksheet on page 16.

Copyright ©2008 Vernon Williams. All rights reserved.

2

SPEND MONEY IN ACCORDANCE WITH YOUR GOALS

Your spending habits must line up with your goals. The best way to make sure this happens is to allocate your income on paper before receiving each paycheck. By doing so, you are telling your money where to **go**, instead of wondering where it **went.**

Activity

a. **Get your next pay stub. (To gain practice while waiting for your next pay day, use your last pay stub).**

b. **Remove a copy of the Income Allocation Worksheet on page 21.**

c. **Record your income and expenses onto the Income Allocation Worksheet (See the line-by-line instructions that follow).**

d. **Repeat step "c" each time you get paid. (Record the information under each succeeding pay day column)**

1. Gross Income

- Regular salary plus bonuses

- Overtime

- Other Income (child support, alimony, rent, interest, dividends, loan repayment, Social Security, SSI, pension, annuity, etc.)

2. Taxes/Other Deductions

- Federal taxes

- State taxes

- FICA taxes - Federal Insurance Contributions Act, which funds Social Security

- Other deductions – union dues, United Givers Fund, long term care, life insurance, etc.

3. Savings/Investments – 401(k), Thrift Savings Plan, U.S. Savings Bonds, etc. Pay yourself first by having savings deducted from your paycheck.

4. Net Income – Line 1 minus lines 2 and 3

Line 5 through 40:

a. Review each line. If you spend money on an item not shown, line through an item that you do not spend money on and write in the item that you spend money on.

b. Determine your number of pay days per year. Let's say you have 26.

c. Determine the amount you spend on each line **per year**. Let's say you pay $180 per month for gas/electric/heating, which equals $2160 for the year. Let's also say you pay $350 semi-annually for auto insurance, which equals $700 for the year.

d. Divide $2160 by 26, which equals $83. Divide $700 by 26, which equals $27.

e. Enter $83 on line 9 – Gas/electric/heating. Enter $27 on line 18 - insurance.

f. Repeat steps c. and d. and enter the amount on the appropriate line of the Income Allocation Worksheet.

g. Deposit that amount into the savings account Line 31 – Savings. This is the "Parking Place" to hold money until payment is due.

Notes:

1. If a bill is due right now, pay it and write the amount you paid on the appropriate line.

2. On the next pay day, write the annual amount divided by your number of pay days on the appropriate line.

3. Follow step "g." above.

5. Contributions to your church -

6. Mortgage (or rent) payment –

7. Insurance – If homeowner insurance is not part of your mortgage payment, list it here. If renting, included renters' insurance here.

8. Taxes – If property taxes are not part of mortgage payment, list them here.

9. Gas/electric/heating-

10. Water/sewage –

11. Telephone – Charges for local and long distance service for the landline in your house/apartment

12. Cell Phone – Monthly access and usage charges, taxes, governmental surcharges and fees

13. Internet access –

14. Maintenance – The amount to be set aside to pay for repairs as they occur

15. Groceries – Food eaten at home

16. Car Payments -

17. Gas & oil – For your car(s)

18. Insurance – Personal injury protection, collision and comprehensive and liability coverage on your car

19. Tags/taxes – License plates/stickers and personal property taxes

20. Inspection – The emission inspection and/or safety inspection required by some jurisdictions

21. Maintenance – Routine (oil change, tune-up, etc.) replacements (tires, belts, batteries) plus unexpected repairs

22. Commuting – Carpool, vanpool, public transportation, commuter bus, etc.

23. Parking/tolls - If you drive to school/work

24. Life Insurance – Premiums

25. Health Insurance – Premiums

26. Other Insurance – Premiums for disability insurance, cancer insurance, etc.

27. Credit card payments –

28. Loan payments – Student loans, finance company, etc.

29. Entertainment
- Eating out/take-out meals –
- Trips –
- Babysitters -
- Movies, video rentals, sporting events, concerts, etc.
- Cable/Satellite TV
- Activities – Bowling, movies concerts, zoo, other sports
- Subscriptions – Newspapers, magazines and journals
- Hobbies/crafts – Bowling, photography, model airplanes, etc.

- Beer, wine, liquor -

- Tobacco products -

- Vacation -

30. Clothing – Purchases of clothing, dry-cleaning, laundry

31. Savings – This is the parking place to hold money pending payment of a bill. When payment is due, transfer the correct amount to your checking account and write a check.

32. Emergency Fund – A job loss, an illness, injury, or a major repair could wreck your spending plan. Establish a separate savings account in case something unexpected happens. The goal is to eventually have at least 3 months of living expenses in the account.

33. Medical -

- Doctors – Office visits

- Dentist – Office visits

- Prescription and over-the-counter drugs/co-pays/deductibles

34. Toiletries - Deodorant, toothpaste, make-up, lotion, etc.

35. Household – Lawn care, cleaning supplies, paper towels, toilet tissue, etc.

   Gifts - Birthday, holiday, graduation, baby shower, anniversary, etc.

36. Grooming - Beauty salon, barber shop, nails, etc.

37. Allowance/lunches - Allowance for children/lunch for adults

38. Cash-husband/wife – Money to spend as one chooses without having to explain

39. Child care/Babysitter – Day care, after school care

40. Education – Tuition, books, fees

41. Total - Lines 5 through 40. Line 41 and line 4 should be the same

See a sample of a completed Income Allocation Worksheet on page 9.

SAMPLE INCOME ALLOCATION WORKSHEET

Category	Pay* Day 1	Pay* Day	Pay* Day	Pay* Day	Pay* Day	Pay* Day	Pay* Day	Pay* Day	Pay* Day	Pay* Day
1. Gross Income	2183									
2. Taxes/Other Ded	297									
3. Savings/Investment	50									
4 .Net Income	1836									
5. Church	100									
6. Mortgage/Rent	800									
7. Insurance										
8.Taxes										
9. Gas/Electric/Heating	166									
10. Water/Sewage	45									
11. Telephone	23									
12.Cell	39									
13.Cable/Internet										
14. Maintenance	15									
15. Groceries	210									
16. Car Payment(s)										
17. Gas & Oil	100									
18. Insurance	30									
19. Tags/Taxes	5									
20. Inspection	5									
21. Maintenance	10									
22. Commuting										
23. Parking/Tolls										
24. Life Insurance	70									
25. Health Ins	40									
26. Other Ins										
27. Credit Cards	30									
28. Loans										
29. Entertainment	15									
30. Clothing/Dry Clean	10									
31. Savings	43									
32. Emergency Fund	20									
33. Medical										
34. Toiletries	10									
35. Household/Gifts										
36. Grooming										
37. Allowance/Lunch	30									
38. Cash-H/W	20									
39. Child Care/Babysitter										
40. Education										
41. Total	1836									

Note: In the "Pay Day" column, write which pay day it is for the year, i.e. 1, 2, 3, etc.

Copyright © 2008 Vernon Williams. All rights reserved.

3

CUT EXPENSES

In order to achieve financial success you must spend less than you earn. This is true whether you earn $15,000 a year or $1 million. Here are some ideas to help you cut expenses:

a. Examine each line on your Income Allocation Worksheet to see if you can reduce or eliminate the expenditure.

Do you really need cable? Can you go to a lower cost (prepaid) cell phone plan? Can you eliminate your landline telephone?

b. Use cash.

According to a Dun & Bradstreet study, **people spend 12-18% more when using credit cards than when using cash**. McDonald's found that the average transaction rose from $4.50 to $7.00 when customers used plastic instead of cash. Why? Because using a credit card doesn't feel like you are spending "Real" money.

c. Ask tough questions when considering a purchase:

- Do I really need this item?

- Is there another, less costly option? (For example, can I purchase a used car instead of a new one?)

- How does purchasing this item impact my achieving my goals?

- Will purchasing this item negatively affect my spending plan this month?

- Will this item be available in the future for a better price? Can I wait?

- Can I purchase this item at a lower price at another retailer or online?

d. Use the envelope system.

People used to use cash envelopes to control their monthly spending. It can still work for certain items. Steps to implementing the system:

1) Decide how much you are going to spend on food, gas, groceries, gifts, clothing and entertainment **each year**.

2) Divide that amount by your number of pay days. See b., c., d., e. under instructions for line 5 through 40 for the Income Allocation Worksheet on pages 5 and 6.

3) Create an envelope for each of the following categories: food, gas, groceries, gifts, clothing and entertainment.

4) Each pay day, deposit the amount you have decided you will spend into the appropriate envelope. For example, if you allow $500 per year for clothing, and you have 26 pay days per year, put $19.23 in cash in your clothing envelope each pay day. ($500.00 divided by 26 = $19.23)

5) Once you've spent all the money in the clothes envelope, (for example) you can't buy any more clothes, unless you take money from another category. Do not go to the ATM or use your credit card.

e. Keep your goals visible.

If your goal is to buy a house, for example, get a picture of the type of house you want. Place the picture in a highly visable area, such as on the refrigerator door. The visual stimulation will keep you inspired to succeed and will help guide your spending decisions.

f. Wipe out credit card debt.

1. Stop using the card(s) that you want to pay off.

Trying to pay off a credit card while continuing to use it is like fighting a war to achieve peace. You can't get there from here.

2. Negotiate a lower Annual Percentage Rate (APR).

Most card issuers are willing to give you a lower rate, particularly if you tell them you have a lower offer from another card issuer. A lower APR obviously means that more of your payment goes to reduce the principle.

3. Ask the card issuer to waive the annual fee.

There is no reason to pay an annual fee for the privilege of paying an average APR of 14%.

4. Make a payment every two weeks.

Interest on an unpaid balance accumulates daily. Because federal law requires credit card issuers to apply payments the day they arrive, the sooner you get your payment in the less interest you pay. In effect, you are using the credit card issuer's strategy (daily interest) against them. Here's how it works: Let's say your minimum payment of $200 is due on the 27th of the month. You can make a payment of $100 on the 1st and a payment of $100 on the 15th. If you do that regularly, you will see the balance drop dramatically.

5. Pay more than the minimum.

Let us say that you have a credit card balance of $3,000 with an APR of 18 percent.

The minimum monthly payment is 2% of the unpaid balance, $60.

By paying $60. per month, at the end of 8 years when the balance is paid in full, you will have paid $5,780. Remember, the original balance was $3,000.

If you pay $110 each month:

You will pay off the balance in 3 years.

The total payments would equal $3,980, which is a savings of **$1,800** ($5780 - $3980).

6. Pay on time.

The average late fee more than doubled between 1992 and 2000, from $12.53 to $27.61. In addition, many credit card issuers will raise the interest rate on your card if you are late. Plan on mailing your payment at least 7 to 10 days before it is due.

7. Read your statement every month.

A recent study showed that 26% of Americans ages 35 to 44 are not aware of their card's interest rate, and 17% fail to review their monthly card statements. As Pete Seeger said, "Education is what you get when you read the fine print. Experience is what you get when you don't." So, read the fine print.

g. Get a copy of *425 Ways to Stretch Your $$$$*. Go to <u>www.howtocutyourexpenses.com.</u>

h. Distinguish between needs and wants.

It is easy to confuse wants with needs.

How many times have you said "I **need** (fill in the blank)" when, in fact, you meant "I **want** (fill in the blank)?"

Let's look at some examples:

Example: "I **need** a new car to get to work." "I **want** a new a new car to get to work."

The **need** could be met by walking, bicycling, carpooling/vanpooling, public transportation, or by buying a used car. Instead, you may choose to satisfy the **want** by buying a new Lexus.

Example: I **need** some slacks. I **want** some designer slacks.

The **need** could be met by purchasing a regular pair of slacks. Instead, you may choose to satisfy the **want** by buying the more expensive designer brand.

Need: Something necessary to maintain life. Examples:

- Air
- Food
- Water
- Shelter
- Sleep
- Clothes
- A job to pay for needs
- Transportation to get to a job (to pay for needs)
- A way to protect one's family in case the breadwinner dies (Life Insurance) or becomes disabled (Disability Income Protection)

Want: Something you would like to have. Examples:

- Luxury car
- Designer clothes
- Smart cell phone
- Big screen TV
- 500 cable channels

Activity

Complete the Needs Vs. Wants Quiz on page 14.

NEEDS VS. WANTS QUIZ

Determine if each item is a need or a want.

Item	Need	Want
Food		
Ice Cream		
Cell Phone		
Designer Clothes		
Life Insurance		
House Payment/Rent		
Big Screen TV		
Eating Out		
Gas/Electricity/Water		
Concert/Movie Tickets		
Disability Insurance		
Magazine/Newspaper Subscription		
Home Box Office (HBO)		
Daily Expresso		
Luxury Car		
Lottery Ticket		
Luxury House/Apartment		
Computer		
CD Player		

Note: Distinguishing between needs and wants does not mean that you should never satisfy wants. Treat yourself to some wants. However, for each dollar you spend on a want; place a dollar into savings for your future. By doing so, you are making sure that satisfying wants does not prevent you from achieving financial success.

Copyright © 2008 Vernon Williams. All rights reserved.

APPENDIX

GOALS WORKSHEET

(**S**pecific) I will _____.

(**M**easurable) I will have achieved my goal when _____.

(**A**chievable) I have the following resources: _____.

I will take the following action:

Action	Complete by
1. _____	_____
2. _____	_____
3. _____	_____
4. _____	_____
5. _____	_____
6. _____	_____
7. _____	_____
8. _____	_____
9. _____	_____
10. _____	_____

(**R**elevant) This goal is meaningful to me because _____.

(**T**ime Definite) I will have achieved my goal by _____.

Copyright ©2008 Vernon Williams. All rights reserved

GOALS WORKSHEET

(**S**pecific) I will _____.

(**M**easurable) I will have achieved my goal when _____.

(**A**chievable) I have the following resources: _____.

I will take the following action:

Action   **Complete by**

1. _____   _____

2. _____   _____

3. _____   _____

4. _____   _____

5. _____   _____

6. _____   _____

7. _____   _____

8. _____   _____

9. _____   _____

10. _____   _____

(**R**elevant) This goal is meaningful to me because _____.

(**T**ime Definite) I will have achieved my goal by _____.

Copyright ©2008 Vernon Williams. All rights reserved

GOALS WORKSHEET

(**S**pecific) I will _____.

(**M**easurable) I will have achieved my goal when _____.

(**A**chievable) I have the following resources: _____.

I will take the following action:

Action   **Complete by**

1. _____   _____

2. _____   _____

3. _____   _____

4. _____   _____

5. _____   _____

6. _____   _____

7. _____   _____

8. _____   _____

9. _____   _____

10. _____   _____

(**R**elevant) This goal is meaningful to me because _____.

(**T**ime Definite) I will have achieved my goal by _____.

Copyright ©2008 Vernon Williams. All rights reserved

18

GOALS WORKSHEET

(**S**pecific) I will _____.

(**M**easurable) I will have achieved my goal when _____.

(**A**chievable) I have the following resources: _____.

I will take the following action:

Action	**Complete by**
1. _____	_____
2. _____	_____
3. _____	_____
4. _____	_____
5. _____	_____
6. _____	_____
7. _____	_____
8. _____	_____
9. _____	_____
10. _____	_____

(**R**elevant) This goal is meaningful to me because _____.

(**T**ime Definite) I will have achieved my goal by _____.

Copyright ©2008 Vernon Williams. All rights reserved

GOALS WORKSHEET

(**S**pecific) I will _____.

(**M**easurable) I will have achieved my goal when _____.

(**A**chievable) I have the following resources: _____.

I will take the following action:

Action   **Complete by**

1. _____   _____

2. _____   _____

3. _____   _____

4. _____   _____

5. _____   _____

6. _____   _____

7. _____   _____

8. _____   _____

9. _____   _____

10. _____   _____

(**R**elevant) This goal is meaningful to me because _____.

(**T**ime Definite) I will have achieved my goal by _____.

Copyright ©2008 Vernon Williams. All rights reserved

INCOME ALLOCATION WORKSHEET

Category	Pay* Day 1	Pay* Day	Pay* Day	Pay* Day	Pay* Day	Pay* Day	Pay* Day	Pay* Day	Pay* Day	Pay* Day
1. Gross Income										
2. Taxes/Other Ded										
3. Savings/Investment										
4 .Net Income										
5. Church										
6. Mortgage/Rent										
7. Insurance										
8.Taxes										
9. Gas/Electric/Heating										
10. Water/Sewage										
11. Telephone										
12.Cell Phone										
13.Cable/Internet										
14. Maintenance										
15. Groceries										
16. Car Payment(s)										
17. Gas & Oil										
18. Insurance										
19. Tags/Taxes										
20. Inspection										
21. Maintenance										
22. Commuting										
23. Parking/Tolls										
24. Life Insurance										
25. Health Ins										
26. Other Ins										
27. Credit Cards										
28. Loans										
29. Entertainment										
30. Clothing/Dry Clean										
31. Savings										
32. Emergency Fund										
33. Medical										
34. Toiletries										
35. Household/Gifts										
36. Grooming										
37. Allowance/Lunch										
38. Cash-H/W										
39. Child Care/Babysitter										
40. Education										
41. Total										

Note: In the "Pay Day" column, write which pay day it is for the year, i.e. 1, 2, 3, etc.

Copyright © 2008 Vernon Williams. All rights reserved.

INCOME ALLOCATION WORKSHEET

Category	Pay* Day 1	Pay* Day	Pay* Day	Pay* Day	Pay* Day	Pay* Day	Pay* Day	Pay* Day	Pay* Day	Pay* Day
1. Gross Income										
2. Taxes/Other Ded										
3. Savings/Investment										
4 .Net Income										
5. Church										
6. Mortgage/Rent										
7. Insurance										
8.Taxes										
9. Gas/Electric/Heating										
10. Water/Sewage										
11. Telephone										
12.Cell Phone										
13.Cable/Internet										
14. Maintenance										
15. Groceries										
16. Car Payment(s)										
17. Gas & Oil										
18. Insurance										
19. Tags/Taxes										
20. Inspection										
21. Maintenance										
22. Commuting										
23. Parking/Tolls										
24. Life Insurance										
25. Health Ins										
26. Other Ins										
27. Credit Cards										
28. Loans										
29. Entertainment										
30. Clothing/Dry Clean										
31. Savings										
32. Emergency Fund										
33. Medical										
34. Toiletries										
35. Household/Gifts										
36. Grooming										
37. Allowance/Lunch										
38. Cash-H/W										
39. Child Care/Babysitter										
40. Education										
41. Total										

Note: In the "Pay Day" column, write which pay day it is for the year, i.e. 1, 2, 3, etc.

Copyright © 2008 Vernon Williams. All rights reserved.

INCOME ALLOCATION WORKSHEET

Category	Pay* Day 1	Pay* Day	Pay* Day	Pay* Day	Pay* Day	Pay* Day	Pay* Day	Pay* Day	Pay* Day	Pay* Day
1. Gross Income										
2. Taxes/Other Ded										
3. Savings/Investment										
4 .Net Income										
5. Church										
6. Mortgage/Rent										
7. Insurance										
8.Taxes										
9. Gas/Electric/Heating										
10. Water/Sewage										
11. Telephone										
12.Cell Phone										
13.Cable/Internet										
14. Maintenance										
15. Groceries										
16. Car Payment(s)										
17. Gas & Oil										
18. Insurance										
19. Tags/Taxes										
20. Inspection										
21. Maintenance										
22. Commuting										
23. Parking/Tolls										
24. Life Insurance										
25. Health Ins										
26. Other Ins										
27. Credit Cards										
28. Loans										
29. Entertainment										
30. Clothing/Dry Clean										
31. Savings										
32. Emergency Fund										
33. Medical										
34. Toiletries										
35. Household/Gifts										
36. Grooming										
37. Allowance/Lunch										
38. Cash-H/W										
39. Child Care/Babysitter										
40. Education										
41. Total										

Note: In the "Pay Day" column, write which pay day it is for the year, i.e. 1, 2, 3, etc.

Copyright © 2008 Vernon Williams. All rights reserved.

INCOME ALLOCATION WORKSHEET

Category	Pay* Day 1	Pay* Day	Pay* Day	Pay* Day	Pay* Day	Pay* Day	Pay* Day	Pay* Day	Pay* Day	Pay* Day
1. Gross Income										
2. Taxes/Other Ded										
3. Savings/Investment										
4 .Net Income										
5. Church										
6. Mortgage/Rent										
7. Insurance										
8.Taxes										
9. Gas/Electric/Heating										
10. Water/Sewage										
11. Telephone										
12.Cell Phone										
13.Cable/Internet										
14. Maintenance										
15. Groceries										
16. Car Payment(s)										
17. Gas & Oil										
18. Insurance										
19. Tags/Taxes										
20. Inspection										
21. Maintenance										
22. Commuting										
23. Parking/Tolls										
24. Life Insurance										
25. Health Ins										
26. Other Ins										
27. Credit Cards										
28. Loans										
29. Entertainment										
30. Clothing/Dry Clean										
31. Savings										
32. Emergency Fund										
33. Medical										
34. Toiletries										
35. Household/Gifts										
36. Grooming										
37. Allowance/Lunch										
38. Cash-H/W										
39. Child Care/Babysitter										
40. Education										
41. Total										

Note: In the "Pay Day" column, write which pay day it is for the year, i.e. 1, 2, 3, etc.

Copyright © 2008 Vernon Williams. All rights reserved.

INCOME ALLOCATION WORKSHEET

Category	Pay* Day 1	Pay* Day	Pay* Day	Pay* Day	Pay* Day	Pay* Day	Pay* Day	Pay* Day	Pay* Day	Pay* Day
1. Gross Income										
2. Taxes/Other Ded										
3. Savings/Investment										
4 .Net Income										
5. Church										
6. Mortgage/Rent										
7. Insurance										
8.Taxes										
9. Gas/Electric/Heating										
10. Water/Sewage										
11. Telephone										
12.Cell Phone										
13.Cable/Internet										
14. Maintenance										
15. Groceries										
16. Car Payment(s)										
17. Gas & Oil										
18. Insurance										
19. Tags/Taxes										
20. Inspection										
21. Maintenance										
22. Commuting										
23. Parking/Tolls										
24. Life Insurance										
25. Health Ins										
26. Other Ins										
27. Credit Cards										
28. Loans										
29. Entertainment										
30. Clothing/Dry Clean										
31. Savings										
32. Emergency Fund										
33. Medical										
34. Toiletries										
35. Household/Gifts										
36. Grooming										
37. Allowance/Lunch										
38. Cash-H/W										
39. Child Care/Babysitter										
40. Education										
41. Total										

Note: In the "Pay Day" column, write which pay day it is for the year, i.e. 1, 2, 3, etc.

Copyright © 2008 Vernon Williams. All rights reserved.

Breinigsville, PA USA
12 February 2010
232380BV00002B/1/P

9 780977 733866